BAKERSFIELD MIST

BAKERSFIELD MIST
by Stephen Sachs

JOSEF WEINBERGER PLAYS

LONDON

BAKERSFIELD MIST
First published in 2014
by Josef Weinberger Ltd
12-14 Mortimer Street, London W1T 3JJ
www.josef-weinberger.com / plays@jwmail.co.uk

Copyright © 2011, 2014 by Stephen Sachs

The Author asserts his moral right to be identified as the author of the Play in relation to all such rights as are granted by the Author to the Company under the terms and conditions of this Agreement in accordance with the Copyright, Designs and Patents Act, 1988.

ISBN: 978 0 85676 344 1

This play is protected by Copyright. According to Copyright Law, no public performance or reading of a protected play or part of that play may be given without prior authorization from Josef Weinberger Plays, as agent for the Copyright Owners.

From time to time it is necessary to restrict or even withdraw the rights of certain plays. It is therefore essential to check with us before making a commitment to produce a play.

NO PERFORMANCE MAY BE GIVEN WITHOUT A LICENCE

AMATEUR PRODUCTIONS
Royalties are due at least one calendar month prior to the first performance. A royalty quotation will be issued upon receipt of the following details:

Name of Licensee
Play Title
Place of Performance
Dates and Number of Performances
Audience Capacity and ticket price(s)

PROFESSIONAL PRODUCTIONS
All enquiries regarding professional rights (excluding First Class rights) should be addressed to Josef Weinberger Plays at the address above. All other enquiries should be addressed to the Susan Gurman Agency LLC, 1501 Broadway, 30th Floor, New York NY, 10036-5601, USA.

OVERSEAS PRODUCTIONS
Applications for productions overseas should be made to our local authorised agents. Further information can be found on our website or in our printed Catalogue of Plays.

CONDITIONS OF SALE
This book is sold subject to the condition that it shall not by way of trade or otherwise be re-sold, hired out, circulated or distributed without prior consent of the Publisher. **Reproduction of the text either in whole or part and by any means is strictly forbidden.**

Printed by Commercial Colour Press plc, Hainault, Essex

BAKERSFIELD MIST was first presented in the UK at the Duchess Theatre, London on 27th May 2014. It was produced by Nica Burns and Sonia Friedman Productions in association with TC Beech Ltd, Tulchin Bartner Productions, Chris & Kelbe Bensinger, Darren Bagert/Martin Massman/ShadowCatcher Entertainment. The cast was as follows:

MAUDE GUTMAN	Kathleen Turner
LIONEL PERCY	Ian McDiarmid

Directed by Polly Teale

Designed by Tom Piper

Lighting designed by Oliver Fenwick

BAKERSFIELD MIST received its world premiere at the Fountain Theatre, Los Angeles on 11th June 2011. It was produced by Simon Levy and Deborah Lawlor for the Fountain Theatre and the National New Play Network. The cast was as follows:

MAUDE GUTMAN	Jenny O'Hara
LIONEL PERCY	Nick Ullett

Directed by Stephen Sachs

Set design by Jeff McLaughlin

Costumes designed by Shon LeBlanc

Lighting designed by Ken Booth

NOTE: The following billing must appear on the title page in every programme and publication under control of each licensee in size and type no less than 75% (seventy five) percent the size of the Author's name:

"BAKERSFIELD MIST was first presented on stage in the United Kingdom by Nica Burns and Sonia Friedman Productions in association with TC Beech Ltd, Tulchin Bartner Productions, Chris & Kelbe Bensinger, Darren Bagert/Martin Massman/ ShadowCatcher Entertainment"

"The World Premiere of BAKERSFIELD MIST was produced at The Fountain Theatre, Los Angeles, directed by Stephen Sachs"

AUTHOR'S NOTE

Inspired, in part, by true events. Bakersfield Mist is a work of fiction. Although inspired in part by a true incident, the characters and events in the play are fictionalized and are not intended to accurately depict or resemble any actual person or event, living or dead. Names, characters, places and incidents have been changed for dramatic purposes.

CHARACTERS

Maude Gutman – unemployed bartender

Lionel Percy – art expert

TIME AND PLACE

A trailer park in Bakersfield, CA.

The trailer home of Maude Gutman.

Present day.

A trailer park in Bakersfield, California. Afternoon. Lights up. The trailer home of MAUDE GUTMAN. *Her trailer home is uniquely furnished with an odd assortment of thrift store artifacts. Odds-and-ends, bric-a-brac. Bizarre lamps. A collection of bottles. A pile of newspapers. Cluttered.* MAUDE *sits at a table drinking Jack Daniels from a shot glass. She fires up a Camel. She grips a letter in her hand. Studies it. Thinks. Struggles. Takes a hit on her Camel. Blows out the smoke. A sudden sound of barking dogs outside.*

MAUDE   Shit.

           (*A cacophony of barking dogs howl and yap outside her trailer front door.* MAUDE *quickly stashes the letter in a tin box. She dashes to the door. Flings it open.*)

MAUDE   (*screaming outside to the dogs*) Get the fuck outta here! You hear me? Get the fuck outta here! (*To her visitor outside.*) No, sir. Not you. I'm talking to the – (*To the barking dogs.*) Will you get the fuck outta here? (*To her visitor.*) Just stand there. Don't move. They won't bite if you don't move. If you move, they're gonna – (*More barking.*) You moved. (*She hollers outside to a neighbor.*) Roberta! Get your fucking dogs! I got somebody over here! Get your dogs or I'll get my gun and blow their fucking brains out!

           (*Sound of dogs barking. Dogs yelping, being pulled away. Barking dogs swirling off into the distance.*)

MAUDE   (*to her visitor outside*) Okay! Come on in!

(LIONEL PERCY *stumbles in through the front door. An elegant, refined gray-haired gentleman in his sixties. A very expensive tailored suit. Clutching an expensive briefcase. He is shaking, terrified.*)

MAUDE I keep telling Roberta those dogs are gonna kill somebody. Who listens to me? Right? Nobody. Come on in. Sit down.

(*He doesn't move.*)

MAUDE They only bark like that when strangers come. We don't get many visitors here. Have a seat. Relax.

(LIONEL *glances at the nearest chair – a bizarre-looking, oddly colored monstrosity.*)

MAUDE Roberta never had kids of her own. The dogs are her babies. Spoils 'em rotten. They eat at the kitchen table with her. Can you believe it? At the table. In chairs. Hamburger. Pork chops.

LIONEL Water.

MAUDE The water she puts in a bowl on the floor.

LIONEL May I please have a –

MAUDE – Oh, yeah – My manners. Out the fucking window. (*Getting a glass, going to the sink.*) I'm nervous. Gotta tell ya. You coming all the way out here. Across the country. I've waited so long. Now you're here. Can't hardly believe it.

LIONEL Neither can I.

MAUDE	My whole life can change in the next thirty seconds. (*Holds out her hand.*) I'm shaking.
LIONEL	I'm having a seizure.
MAUDE	(*at the sink, looking out the window*) Who's the gent outside?
LIONEL	The driver.
MAUDE	Bring him in.
LIONEL	The dogs have persuaded him to stay in the car.
MAUDE	I don't want him waiting out there by himself.
LIONEL	(*eyeing her bizarre place*) Don't worry. This won't take long.

(*She brings him the glass of water.*)

MAUDE	Here ya go. (*Holds up her glass of Jack Daniels.*) You want a little something else 'sides water?
LIONEL	I'm working.
MAUDE	It'll take the edge off.
LIONEL	I'll keep the edge on, if you don't mind.
MAUDE	Any trouble finding the place?
LIONEL	Actually, yes. The address of your trailer park didn't appear on the limo's navigational system.

MAUDE	Hah! That's us. Off the beaten path. How was your flight?
LIONEL	I'm here.
MAUDE	What was the movie?
LIONEL	No movie.
MAUDE	All the way from New York? No movie?
LIONEL	I'm afraid not.
MAUDE	Fucking airlines. Cutting everything. I flew to Des Moines to visit my cousin Frannie 'cause of her gall bladder. They charged me for a pillow. Can you believe it? A fucking pillow! Next they'll run your credit card every time you go to the toilet. Don't get me started. What you fly? Sounds like Delta.
LIONEL	The Foundation has a jet.
MAUDE	Oh.
LIONEL	Shall we get down to business?
MAUDE	Yeah. All right.
LIONEL	The Foundation assigned me as the consulting expert on this case. I, of course, am Lionel Percy.
MAUDE	Maude Gutman.
LIONEL	You know who I am.
MAUDE	I hit the fucking jackpot.

LIONEL	There is a long list of small-time mediocre art experts.
MAUDE	I bet.
LIONEL	I am not on that list.
MAUDE	I gotta thank you. Taking my case. Flying all the way out here. Such an important, busy man. You must have better things to do.
LIONEL	You have no idea.
MAUDE	Why did they assign you to my painting, do you think?
LIONEL	I now teach Abstract Expressionism at Princeton University. Prior to that, for twelve years I served as curator, and then director, for the Metropolitan Museum of Art. (*A look to her.*) That's in New York City. (*Organizing his paperwork.*) After leaving the Met, for seven years I was editor-in-chief at *Connoisseur* magazine.
MAUDE	Never read it.
LIONEL	(*glancing about the room*) Indeed. (*Then.*) In addition to teaching, I now serve on the Board at the Whitney, the Frick and the Museum of Modern Art. I am a lecturer. The author of several books. Two on the Times best seller list. Many now considered classic texts. "The History of Art in Western Civilization", "The Chronology of Modern Art in America", "The Symbolist Aesthetics of Abstract Expressionism". (*Directly at her.*) "Art for Dummies".

MAUDE	Can I get you a beer?
LIONEL	No, thank you.

(*She bolts up.*)

MAUDE	Shit! I nearly forgot! I made a little something. You hungry?
LIONEL	No.
MAUDE	Nothing fancy.
LIONEL	I was about to say –
MAUDE	You look thin. You should eat.

(*She fetches the plate.*)

LIONEL	(*trying to stay on topic*) The International Foundation for Art Research –
MAUDE	Just a little nibble.
LIONEL	– is a world class –
MAUDE	A little whatcha-call-it.
LIONEL	– recognized world-wide as the foremost art organization –
MAUDE	(*presenting the tray before him*) Ta-da! Here ya go. (*Proud.*) Don't be shy. Help yourself. They're little wiener rolls. I made them myself. (*Pointing.*) With Velveeta. (*Pointing.*) Without.

(*A beat.*)

LIONEL	Perhaps later.

MAUDE	Should I get the painting now?
LIONEL	Paperwork first. Shall we? (*Pulling folders from his briefcase.*) Among its many goals, The Foundation for Art Research strives to prevent the circulation of forged, misattributed, or misappropriated art. Disproving forgeries is a personal crusade of mine. I like to think of myself as a fakebuster.
MAUDE	My painting is not a fake.
LIONEL	Well, if you're the expert, then what am I doing here?
MAUDE	I need you.
LIONEL	How flattering.
MAUDE	We'll see.
LIONEL	The Foundation draws on an international network of art scholars and experts from around the world, of global eminence – that would be me – to provide expertise to the public. That would be you. To verify the authenticity of works of art. We only accept a very limited number of projects like this each year. We receive hundreds of applications. From all over the world. Few are chosen.
MAUDE	You must really think my painting is real.
	(*He opens her file.*)
LIONEL	Your application. The two color photographs you sent of the painting. A photocopy of the

non-refundable deposit. The full balance of the fee. The name on your checks: he is?

MAUDE My brother.

LIONEL I see.

MAUDE I don't have the money for any of this.

LIONEL Is there a Mister Gutman?

MAUDE There was.

LIONEL Was?

MAUDE He's gone.

LIONEL Dead?

MAUDE Let's hope.

LIONEL And how long have you resided here at . . . Sagebrush Trailer Park?

MAUDE Thirty-three years.

LIONEL By yourself?

MAUDE Sometimes. (*A sly wink at him.*) Sometimes not.

(*She gives him an "if you catch my drift" kind of look.*)

LIONEL Occupation?

MAUDE Bartender.

LIONEL Of course.

MAUDE   Was.

LIONEL   I see.

MAUDE   They fired me. I quit.

           (*She downs her drink. Refills her glass.*)

LIONEL   You are certainly not the standard art collector I typically encounter.

MAUDE   This is me, pal.

LIONEL   (*a smug chuckle*) I hardly see you sipping Clos du Mesnil with Diane Von Furstenberg at Acquavella evaluating de Kooning.

           (*He chuckles at his own joke.*)

MAUDE   I'd rather stay home with a sixer and watch *Dancing with the Stars*. Can I bring in the fucking painting now?

           (*He hands her documents.*)

LIONEL   I need you to sign this agreement.

MAUDE   What's it say?

LIONEL   That you fully understand that my job is to render an objective expert opinion on the authenticity of the painting. That I am forbidden from offering you a monetary appraisal.

           (*She stares at him. Blank.*)

LIONEL   If I believe that the painting is authentic, I can not tell you how much the painting may be worth. Do you understand?

MAUDE   I understand.

LIONEL   I have no interest whatsoever in this outcome.

MAUDE   Okay.

LIONEL   Do you understand?

MAUDE   Yeah. Okay.

LIONEL   After seeing and evaluating the painting, I will check one of the two boxes on this form. "Yes" I do believe the painting to be authentic. "No" I do not. A fully written report outlining my findings and stating my opinion as to authenticity and attribution will be mailed to you from New York.

MAUDE   Got it.

LIONEL   Sign here.

(*She starts to sign. Stops.*)

MAUDE   So – how much do you think my painting could be worth?

(*He stares at her.*)

LIONEL   Did you not hear a single word I just said?

MAUDE   I heard.

LIONEL   I am forbidden to –

MAUDE   I know.

LIONEL   The Foundation prohibits me from –

MAUDE	I'm not asking this painting.
LIONEL	Good.
MAUDE	I'm asking in general.
LIONEL	I can't.
MAUDE	In theory.
LIONEL	No.
MAUDE	Before you even see it.
LIONEL	No.
MAUDE	How much?
LIONEL	Mrs Gutman . . .
MAUDE	Call me Maude.
LIONEL	I will not call you Maude.
MAUDE	How much?
LIONEL	I –
MAUDE	Not this painting. A painting like it. What if? Conversation.

(*He glares at her.*)

MAUDE Please. (*Beat.*) Come on. (*Silence.*) Be a person.

(*A long beat.*)

LIONEL	Let me be clear: I am not saying this painting. Do you understand?
MAUDE	I understand.
LIONEL	Not this painting.
MAUDE	No.
LIONEL	But in theory?
MAUDE	Yeah.
LIONEL	A painting like it?
MAUDE	Yeah.
LIONEL	If it is authentic? (*Beat.*) I'm saying if. (*Beat.*) The current market value could be anywhere from . . . (*Hesitates.*) . . . fifty to one hundred million dollars.
	(*Silence. They stare at each other. A very long pause. Then* MAUDE *signs the agreement.*)
LIONEL	The painting is not signed by any artist.
MAUDE	No.
LIONEL	And you know nothing of its provenance.
MAUDE	Its what?
LIONEL	Its provenance. The history of its ownership prior to you.
MAUDE	Who the fuck knows?

LIONEL	Yes. You still have no documentation – no paper trail – linking you and the painting back to the artist?
MAUDE	Listen, pal – I don't know the "pro-van-ahnze" of this thing I got on from the thrift store, forget about the fucking painting.
LIONEL	I see.
MAUDE	That doesn't mean it isn't real.
LIONEL	So the identity of the artist is uncertain.
MAUDE	Not in my mind.
LIONEL	A precarious landscape, to be sure. (*Then.*) Tell again. For the record. How you came upon the painting.
MAUDE	(*the application*) I wrote it all out. In there. How it happened.
LIONEL	Indulge me.
MAUDE	From the horse's mouth, eh?
LIONEL	I was hesitant to use a zoological reference.
MAUDE	In my own . . .
LIONEL	Idiosyncratic vocabulary.
MAUDE	Can't I just get the fucking thing and bring it in?
LIONEL	(*dry, snide*) Please. (*Beat.*) Be a person. (*Beat. She fires up a Camel.*)

MAUDE (*grinning*) Hold on to your hat. This is un-fucking-believable. (*She stands.*) I'm a scavenger. A pack rat. Always going to thrift stores, junk shops, Salvation Army. Finding bargains, picking up shit that other people throw away. (*Proud.*) It may come as a bit of a shock to you. But I've decorated my entire home that way. Everything you see before you here in this room is throwaway stuff. Crap other people toss. Shit I've pulled out from the bottom of dumpsters.

LIONEL (*dry*) Imagine my surprise.

MAUDE (*pouring herself a drink*) So one day, about three years ago, I'm in Daisy's Junk Shop over on Highway 80. Looking for a set of shot glasses to go with that old ice bucket I pulled out of the garbage behind Lenny's Bar & Grill.

LIONEL The establishment that fired you.

MAUDE I quit.

LIONEL My mistake.

MAUDE I'm in Daisy's. And I see some old paintings stacked up against the wall in back by the used paperbacks. Now, my ol' buddy Roberta – she lives in the trailer down the way –

LIONEL With the dogs.

MAUDE Her birthday was the day before. She was bein' an old sour puss, feelin' like an old maid, all sorry for herself – so I figured I'd buy her one of these fucking paintings.

As a joke. Cheer her up. So I look in the stack. For the ugliest one. And I pull out this God-awful piece of shit – I'm thinking, "Man, this is ugly." I take it to the counter. Daisy wants five bucks. But I say, "You see how ugly this thing is? Who else is gonna buy it? I'll give you three." She takes the three. I throw the painting in the back of my truck. Drive it back here. Laughing all the way home. So I give it to Roberta: "Happy Birthday, you ol' bat!" She takes one look at it – goes ballistic. Won't take it. Wants nothing to do with it. So me and Roberta, we – (*Chuckles.*) – we have a few beers. A few more. Before you know it, we grab my .45, take the painting out back of her trailer – we're gonna shoot it full of holes. (*Drinks, laughs.*) But we get so shit-faced we can't find the bullets for my gun so – fuck it – Roberta throws the painting out into the street. She hates the fucking thing. Goes inside. Slams her front door. Now I'm stuck with it. (*Gestures to the bottle of Jack Daniels.*) Sure you don't want any?

LIONEL   No, thank you.

MAUDE   (*pours herself another shot*) A few months later I'm having a yard sale. I put the painting outside. Right out there in my front yard with a bunch of other junk I'm trying to get rid of. And Tom Bucky – he's the art teacher over at MacArthur High School – happens to come by. Looking for an old frying pan or something. He glances over. Sees the painting. Picks it up. Takes a long look at it. Calls me over. And he says to me, "I may be wrong. But this could be a Jackson Pollock."

LIONEL	And you had no idea who Jackson Pollock was.
MAUDE	Not a fucking clue.
LIONEL	And now?
MAUDE	I know. (*She eyes him. Determined.*) I know. (*Beat.*) Can I get the painting now?
LIONEL	Yes. You can get the painting now.

(MAUDE *sets down her drink and darts off into the bedroom.* LIONEL *waits a moment. Peers around the oddly-furnished trailer. He stands, wanders over to a shelf. Spots a framed photo of a young man. Picks it up. Looks at it. Sets it down.*)

MAUDE   (*offstage*) Ready or not! Here it comes!

(MAUDE *enters from the bedroom carrying a large canvas covered with a bed sheet. She places the covered canvas on a chair. She props it up, prepping it. Before revealing the painting – She dashes over and brings a lamp closer to it, for better viewing. Adjusts the lamp, the lighting. She switches the lights off in the room (leaving the lamp on as a "spotlight"). Decides against it. Switches the room lights back on. She "places" a chair for* LIONEL, *a few feet in front of the canvas, for optimum viewing. He sits in the chair. She quickly dashes over and removes a few objects aside in the room, so nothing obstructs or sullies his view. She steps back. Turns to* LIONEL *with a look that asks, "Ready?"* LIONEL *nods, "Ready."* MAUDE *steps forward to the canvas. She reaches up and slowly, dramatically . . . removes the bed sheet from the canvas . . . and steps aside. The painting is revealed. It is a torrent, a tornado, a storm of color. A kaleidoscopic spattering of drips and curves and splattered lines in a vibrant variety of colors. Violent splashes of red and black streak across the canvas like slashing gashes, trickles of green, drips of yellow, vivid spatterings of white and orange.* MAUDE *stares at* LIONEL *in the chair. Her eyes glued on him.* LIONEL *doesn't move. He peers at the painting. Motionless. He then bends his elbow, and carefully places his chin in his palm. His eyes never leave the painting. Studying it.* LIONEL *sits. Frozen. Staring at the painting. He then rises. Stands. His eyes never leaving the painting. He takes a step forward. A step back. From a few feet away, he bends all the way forward, at the waist, and now peers at the painting with his head upside down. He rights himself. Takes two steps forward. He slowly walks up to the painting. Stands directly in front of it. Puts his nose right up to the canvas. Expertly studies the surface. He steps to the side of the painting. Gets a "side view".* LIONEL *stands back. Silence.* MAUDE *waits. A long, long, long pause.*)

LIONEL   It's not a Pollock.

           (*Silence.*)

MAUDE   What?

LIONEL   It's not a Pollock.

MAUDE   You sure?

LIONEL   Of course I'm sure.

MAUDE	How do you know?
LIONEL	I'm an expert. I know.
	(*Beat.*)
LIONEL	I'm going to need you to sign a release form.
MAUDE	Wait a minute. That's it? That's fucking it?
LIONEL	That's it.
MAUDE	How?
LIONEL	We're done.
MAUDE	Wait-wait-wait-wait.
LIONEL	Is there a problem?
MAUDE	Aren't you going to do some tests?
LIONEL	Tests?
MAUDE	Some scientific fucking tests.
LIONEL	I don't need tests.
MAUDE	How can you tell just by looking at it?
LIONEL	It's called connoisseurship.
MAUDE	It's called horse shit.
LIONEL	A connoisseur has expert knowledge. Is one who knows.
MAUDE	So me? I don't know?

LIONEL	You have summoned me to know. It is my job to know.
MAUDE	It may be your job. But it's my fucking life.
LIONEL	Don't raise your voice at me.
MAUDE	What do you expect?
LIONEL	Being impolite will not improve your situation.
MAUDE	I don't mean to be "impolite".
LIONEL	I understand your disappointment.
MAUDE	My "disappointment"?
LIONEL	I'll just complete this form then be on my way.
MAUDE	Please. Just look at it again.
LIONEL	I don't need to look again.
MAUDE	Yes, you do.
LIONEL	No I don't. I knew it. From the first.
MAUDE	From the first?
LIONEL	I always trust my "blink".
MAUDE	Your what?
LIONEL	My "blink".
MAUDE	What the fuck is that? Your "blink"?

LIONEL: The blink of an eye. Rapid cognition. First impression. How a painting hits me. The first two seconds.

MAUDE: Two seconds?

LIONEL: Two seconds. It's called knowing without thinking.

MAUDE: It's called bullshitting without looking.

LIONEL: Let me frame it for you this way: When you meet someone for the first time, or first walk into a house – like this one, for instance – it only takes two seconds to reach a conclusion. You see it. You know. The Blink.

MAUDE: First impressions can be wrong.

LIONEL: Mine aren't.

MAUDE: How can you say that?

LIONEL: Expertise. Scholarship. My blinks are always accurate.

MAUDE: And your blink on my painting was – ?

LIONEL: Intuitive repulsion.

MAUDE: Stand over here. Blink over here.

LIONEL: This painting has no artistic soul.

MAUDE: Maybe if I turn on the lamp.

LIONEL: It distresses me.

MAUDE: Take off your jacket.

LIONEL	I feel disquieted. Unsettled.
MAUDE	Have a drink.
LIONEL	The paint application is tidy. Concise.
MAUDE	That's good.
LIONEL	That's bad.
MAUDE	That's bad?
LIONEL	Pollock was never tidy. Pollock was volcanic. Pollock was explosive. On fire. This . . . (*The painting.*) this is shallow. Empty. It has no allure.
MAUDE	Hey, I don't like the painting either. That doesn't mean it isn't . . .
LIONEL	(*gesturing to a section of the painting*) I mean, look at it. Look at this here. (*Another section.*) And this. (*Another section.*) And this over here. (*Shaking his head.*) Pollock's work always teetered on disaster. Catastrophe. Each canvas was a leap off the cliff. Life or death. Which made them so electrifying, so thrilling. So exhilarating. But this . . . this has no peril, no danger. I look at it. And I'm waiting.
MAUDE	For what?
LIONEL	The tingle. The tingle I get when I know I am standing in the presence of something authentic.

(*They both stare at the painting.*)

MAUDE	Are you tingling?

LIONEL	It is not the work of Jackson Pollock.
	(*He takes an expensive pen out of his breast pocket and "clicks" it.*)
LIONEL	I'm sorry, Mrs Gutman, but I am afraid I am going to have to check the "No" box on my form.
MAUDE	No you're not.
LIONEL	Yes I am.
MAUDE	No, you are not.
LIONEL	Beg your pardon?
MAUDE	You can't.
LIONEL	I know what art is.
MAUDE	I like pictures. Same as you. See? Look. Look at this. Over here.
	(*She points to a picture on her wall. An old thrift store painting of two circus clowns. He stares at her.*)
LIONEL	You're kidding me, right?
MAUDE	What's the matter with it?
LIONEL	That is not art.
MAUDE	It's more art than that. At least this looks like something. You know what it is! A painting is supposed to look like something. Right? (*Her circus clowns.*) This, you look at it? You know what it is.

LIONEL	Yes. Odious repugnancy.
MAUDE	I like it. It's art.
	(*He stares at her.*)
LIONEL	This is ridiculous. If you're just going to contradict my expertise then why did you apply for my approval in the first place?
MAUDE	I need you to say that my painting is real.
LIONEL	But it's not real.
MAUDE	It is.
LIONEL	Every known Pollock is either in a museum or in private collection.
MAUDE	Every known Pollock.
LIONEL	You think a trailer park bartender –
MAUDE	Ex-bartender –
LIONEL	– from Bakersfield can just walk into a junk store and for three bucks buy a masterpiece worth one hundred million dollars?
MAUDE	It happens.
LIONEL	Where? In *The National Enquirer*?
MAUDE	They just found all those Picassos in France. And this other guy in Buffalo. He had a painting crammed behind the family sofa for twenty-seven years.
LIONEL	Martin Kober.

MAUDE	Turns out to be a Michelangelo worth three hundred million.
LIONEL	They're doing infrared and x-rays. It has not been confirmed.
MAUDE	Good can finally hit a person, can't it? Miracles happen. Don't they? God can smile down on you at least once in your fucking life and throw you a blessing?
LIONEL	I am not an expert on God. New York, on the other hand, is never going to approve of this painting. Or of you.
MAUDE	What is that supposed to mean?
LIONEL	The work has no value.
MAUDE	Approve of me?
LIONEL	It has no aesthetic purpose.
MAUDE	I don't give a shit if New York approves of me.
LIONEL	Well, there's a sigh of relief.
MAUDE	What? Someone like me can't own a masterpiece?
LIONEL	My evaluation is not of you.
MAUDE	You don't want it to be a Pollock.
LIONEL	Nothing would thrill me more.
MAUDE	Well, get happy. That painting is real.
LIONEL	It is a forgery.

MAUDE	It's impossible to forge a Pollock.
LIONEL	How would you know?
MAUDE	(*pointing*) Who else would paint shit like that?
LIONEL	Francis Hogan Brown.
MAUDE	Who?
LIONEL	Francis Hogan Brown. An abstract drip-and-splatter painter. Had a studio here in California. Palm Springs. Years ago. Copied Pollock. Painted hundreds of canvases. For thirty years. All copies of Pollock. Sold many right here in this area. They turn up every so often. I suspected this might be a Brown when I first got this assignment. Forgeries are my specialty. My passion. Now that I've seen the painting – I'm sure. It's a Brown.
	(MAUDE *agonizes*.)
MAUDE	This. Is a Pollock. I know it is. I feel it.
LIONEL	It's a Brown.
MAUDE	It is real. It has to be.
LIONEL	No, in fact it doesn't. (*Then.*) Sorry to be the Grim Reaper. The herald of catastrophe. Sounder of the death knell. Crushing your dream of fame and fortune . . .
MAUDE	I don't care about fame and fortune.
LIONEL	Oh, really? One hundred million dollars? Think of the shot glasses . . .

MAUDE	I don't give a shit about the money.
LIONEL	What do you give a "shit" about?
MAUDE	The truth. You snooty son of a bitch.

(*Silence.*)

LIONEL	(*stung*) I see. Well. First you'll have to learn how to accept it. (*Collecting his papers.*) Now, if you'll excuse me I'll take my pen. (*Snapping his briefcase shut.*) I'll complete the paperwork on the ride to the airport.

(*He heads for the door.*)

MAUDE	What if you're wrong?
LIONEL	I'm not wrong.
MAUDE	What if you are? What would happen?
LIONEL	Happen?
MAUDE	To you. If you're wrong.

(*He stops. Turns.*)

LIONEL	What do you mean? What would happen to me?
MAUDE	You fly to New York. Tell the art world the painting is a forgery, a fake. And it turns out to be real. "The find of the century." What would happen?
LIONEL	I don't see the point.
MAUDE	To you. What would happen? To you.

LIONEL	Nothing would happen to me.
MAUDE	You sure? Maybe I should get another expert.
LIONEL	Be my guest. Go ahead.
MAUDE	I will.
LIONEL	Do it. Survey the art world. You'll see. Mine is still the opinion that matters.
MAUDE	Not if you're wrong. Again.
LIONEL	Excuse me?
MAUDE	Huh?
LIONEL	What was that?
MAUDE	You heard me.
LIONEL	How dare you.
MAUDE	I'm just saying.
LIONEL	My standing in the art world is impeccable. Absolute.
MAUDE	You've never been wrong?
LIONEL	No.
MAUDE	Never made a mistake?
LIONEL	No.
MAUDE	A wrong judgement? A wrong conclusion?

LIONEL   Never.

MAUDE   About anything?

LIONEL   Not when it comes to art.

MAUDE   Who's not accepting the truth now?

LIONEL   There is only one truth.

MAUDE   Yours?

LIONEL   Great art. Is the only truth. When the gods speak it's –

         (*Stops himself. Turns to go.*)

MAUDE   What?

LIONEL   Never mind.

MAUDE   When the gods speak what?

LIONEL   I am done. You will receive my report in ten days.

MAUDE   When have the Gods ever spoken to you?

         (*This freezes him at the door. He halts. Doesn't move.*)

LIONEL   I was seventeen. The Museum of Modern Art. A field trip. School.

         (*He stops himself. Clams up. Turns for the door.*)

MAUDE   Go on. A field trip. School.

         (*He halts. Considers. Then, quietly.*)

LIONEL	We got off the bus. Walked in. Up the stairs. Turned the corner. And . . . (*He can't find the words.*) There it was.
MAUDE	What?
	(*Silence.*)
LIONEL	Picasso. *Les Demoiselles d'Avignon.*
	(*She stares at him.*)
LIONEL	It's this big, huge painting. (*Then.*) The canvas attacked like some kind of primitave and savage blue, beige and brown atomic bomb. It was terrifying. I had no idea what I was seeing. "That's ugly" I said to my friend. Then my teacher, Miss Pritchard, put her hand on my shoulder. My left shoulder. Right here. And she said to me: "Lionel, nothing in the entire history of art is like it. It is the single most influential work of art ever created." And she was right. (*Breathes deeply.*) Until Pollock. Pollock stretched Cubism and Surrealism beyond recognition. Picasso was suddenly a painter of the past. Pollock was modern art. He cracked the art world – the art universe – wide open. The splitting of the atom. The flash of a nuclear blast. "Now I am become Death, the destroyer of worlds." He reconfigured the molecular structure of art. You look at his paintings and they rewire your retinas. Movement made infinite. No beginning or end. Each painting just is. (*Moving closer to her. Intense.*) Every great artist paints what he is. Pollock didn't paint from nature. Pollock said, I *am* nature. Primitive. Savage. Pollock said, "I enter each painting as I paint it". He would lay the canvas across the floor like a lover. Lean over it, straddle it . . .

(LIONEL *leans over an imaginary painting, demonstrating.*)

. . . bend over it, tease it, talk to it, mutter to it like a madman – whisper to it – in dialogue with the painting, coaxing it, caressing it, tickling it, teasing it, then . . . enter it!

(*Now pacing wildly like a madman.*)

Hand swirling – spinning – flinging – spattering – circling the canvas, in a trance like a shaman – dripping – pouring his unconscious – a panther on the prowl, the matador stalking the bull, knowing when to strike – then – the assault – violent – explosive – bursts of brush – lariats of color – flinging paint like throwing dice – knowing how the paint would land – a frenzy – swirling lines – lines that curve – dance – explode – lines in teal and raspberry – yellow – an arabesque of amethyst – No brush touching canvas. Never! His body was the brush – creating art in the air – bending paint to fall at his will – he drooled it, spattered it – bleeding on the canvas, ejaculating – cumming on canvas – paintings as fever – art as ecstacy – white heat.

(LIONEL *working himself up into a frenzy.*)

Pollock was Kerouac on canvas: "The only people for me are the mad ones, the ones who are mad to live, mad to talk, mad to be saved, desirous of everything at the same time, the ones who never yawn or say a commonplace thing, but burn, burn, burn like fabulous roman candles exploding like spiders across the stars and in the middle you see the blue centerlight pop and everybody goes 'Awww!'".

(*Silence.* LIONEL *is spent. Perspiring. Out of breath.* MAUDE *stares at him.*)

LIONEL I beg your pardon.

(*He doesn't move. Then* MAUDE *pours a Jack Daniels into a shot glass. Hands it out to* LIONEL. *Offers it to him. He takes the drink. Downs it. She refills his glass. Shakes the bottle. Now empty.*)

MAUDE I got a case I took from Lenny's. My last day.

LIONEL You stole it.

MAUDE Severance pay.

LIONEL Why did they fire you? Sorry. Right. You quit.

(*She looks away. Then.*)

MAUDE I was fired.

LIONEL Why?

MAUDE Because I tried to kill myself.

(MAUDE *dumps the empty bottle of Jack Daniels into a metal trash can. Clang. She exits.* LIONEL *is left alone. He rises. Carries his drink. Slowly crosses to the painting. Drawn to it. He looks at it. Closely. Stares at it. Peers deep into it. He drifts back over to the framed photo of the young man.*

Studies it. Suddenly MAUDE *re-enters. A fresh bottle in her hand.)*

MAUDE   Put that down.

LIONEL   I was just –

MAUDE   Put it down.

(He sets down the framed photo. MAUDE *cracks open the bottle. Lights up a cigarette.)*

MAUDE   I was in here one time. Just me and the painting. Making myself a rum and coke. The painting right there. Where it is now. Like an old friend. I was talking to it. Like I do. Sometimes. When I'm alone. Suddenly . . . outta nowhere . . . the wind picked up outside. Gentle. Those old beer bottle wind chimes out there started to rattle. Come to life. The sun ducked behind a cloud. The sunlight in here shifted, started to move. The light from outside fell on the painting just a certain way. And all of a sudden . . . for a moment . . . it almost kinda looked . . . nice. You know? Kinda beautiful. Alive.

(They stare at the painting.)

LIONEL   They say that Pollock – on some of his drip paintings – actually urinated on some of them. Peed on them. As he painted.

MAUDE   That fucker was crazy.

LIONEL   He drank too much.

MAUDE   He was angry. In pain.

LIONEL	He had demons.
MAUDE	Don't we all.

(He looks at her.)

LIONEL	You really tried to kill yourself?

(Silence. Uncomfortable. Awkward. He regards the painting again.)

LIONEL	When a woman he loved suddenly died Pollock grabbed a knife and slashed up all the paintings he was working on at the time. A kind of suicide. Sliced them up. Threw all the shreds of canvas out the window.
MAUDE	The human heart can be . . .

(Silence. She refills their two glasses.)

MAUDE *(a toast)* Here's to me.

Here's to you.

Here's to those we fuck and screw.

Here's to them for fucking us over,

And here's to us – for never being sober!

(She downs her drink. He does not. Stares at her in disbelief.)

LIONEL	Your turn-of-phrase is . . .
MAUDE	"Maude the Broad". My husband called me. Among other things.
LIONEL	With affection, no doubt.

MAUDE	Are you kidding? That man made me feel like . . . (*Stops herself.*)
LIONEL	You have a son?
MAUDE	(*his glass*) Drink up. Down the fucking hatch.
LIONEL	I shouldn't. I can't.
MAUDE	Why not?
LIONEL	I'm still working.
MAUDE	All work and no play . . .
LIONEL	It's against the rule of professional conduct.
MAUDE	Rules Shmooles! I don't follow rules – I break 'em – and look at me.
LIONEL	My point exactly.
MAUDE	You think Jackson Pollack gave a shit about the rules?
LIONEL	I am not Jackson Pollack.
MAUDE	That's a fucking understatement.

(LIONEL *recoils. Stung. He downs his drink. Sits motionless.* MAUDE *brings the bottle, refilling his glass.*)

MAUDE	I say things. Shit comes out. My social skills need fucking polishing.
LIONEL	(*allowing his glass to be refilled*) I really shouldn't be doing this.

MAUDE   Mum's the word.

LIONEL   This is not how these Foundation assignments are designed to unfold.

MAUDE   You might surprise yourself. Bottoms up.

LIONEL   I don't like surprises.

MAUDE   You ever Google yourself? Your own name?

LIONEL   No, I have never Googled my own name.

MAUDE   Get the fuck outta here.

LIONEL   I haven't.

MAUDE   Yeah? I thought you were your own favorite subject.

(*He glares at her.*)

MAUDE   Oops. See? I did it again.

(*She grabs the bottle.*)

MAUDE   You go to Google. Type my name? Nothing comes up. Zippity-doo-dah. Me and my life, it has "no results". I don't exist. (*Refilling his drink.*) But you. All kinds of shit comes up. You exist.

LIONEL   I existed. Once.

MAUDE   Me and my brother. We Googled you.

LIONEL   Oh?

MAUDE   You betcha. Kit and kaboodle. Back when you started. A long time ago.

LIONEL: I believe it was the Cretaceous Period.

MAUDE: Your first big break.

LIONEL: I was a young curator at the Met. The Modern Art Department.

MAUDE: A little hot-shot even then?

LIONEL: My address book of dealers, collectors, artists, agents, and smugglers was legendary.

MAUDE: How did you get to running the place?

LIONEL: One afternoon, the Museum Director suddenly died.

MAUDE: How?

LIONEL: A cerebral hemorrhage. After a particularly brutal meeting with the Board of Trustees.

MAUDE: Bummer.

LIONEL: A committee was formed. Chaired by the Annenbergs and the Rockefeller Foundation. They searched the world for a successor.

MAUDE: And you were chosen.

LIONEL: I was thirty-six years old. It was December. The finest Christmas present I've ever received.

MAUDE: That museum is like a big fucking place, right?

LIONEL: In the art world, The Metropolitan is like the Vatican.

MAUDE	Out of touch with reality?
LIONEL	A temple of the human spirit. A palace of the soul. A cathedral preserving five thousand years of the artistic expression of Man.
MAUDE	So, if it's like the Vatican, that made you – what? Pope?

(*He is pleased with the comparison.*)

LIONEL	(*a proud grin*) For a while. Yes. I was. The Pope of Fifth Avenue. (*Then.*) To be director of the Metropolitan Museum of Art, one is part Pope, part used car salesman, a gunslinger, publicity whore, art scholar, grave robber, and Papa Bear to a staff of eight hundred.
MAUDE	Where'd you learn to do all that?
LIONEL	I made it up as I went along. Flying around the globe. Exotic sites – ancient tombs, murky catacombs – discovering magnificent treasure.
MAUDE	You were Indiana Jones.
LIONEL	With a much bigger expense account. Lord and Ruler of the Art Universe. They were . . . the most thrilling years of my life.
MAUDE	Until the end. When they fired you.
LIONEL	I quit.
MAUDE	My mistake.
LIONEL	Years ago.

MAUDE	Why did you quit?
LIONEL	I committed the greatest sin in the Museum business.
MAUDE	What's that?
LIONEL	I cared about the art. (*Then.*) One must enter the art world like one enters the priesthood: To serve a higher power. A work of art is both human and spiritual. A painting, a sculpture, a tapestry is a physical thing expressing the non-physical. The beyond-physical. Great art has spiritual power. Embedded within it. The power to cure the heart, heal the human spirit, save and uplift the soul.
MAUDE	I read that they fired you.
LIONEL	The Trustees demanded ever more media-grabbing exhibits. Museum shops. Merchandise. Franchising "Met Stores" into Bloomindale's. Art became "Product". I would have none of it. So I left.
MAUDE	You were fired.
LIONEL	I resigned.
MAUDE	They fired you. Over that boy.
	(LIONEL *freezes.*)
MAUDE	That naked young man.
	(*He doesn't move.*)
MAUDE	Didn't they.

(*Silence.*)

MAUDE That statue.

(*Silence.*)

LIONEL It's called a kouros.

MAUDE Whatever.

LIONEL An Ancient Greek statue. 530 BC. Dolomitic marble. From a quarry in Saliari on Thasos. An island in the North Aegean.

MAUDE You had the Museum buy it for millions of –

LIONEL It was glorious. Free standing. Six feet nine inches tall. Nude. Arms at sides, hands clenched into fists, eyes straight ahead, left foot forward, striding forth with noble beauty. Confident. Unafraid. The idea of youth. The ideal of Greek culture. Arete.

MAUDE Huh?

LIONEL "Arete". Ancient Greek for something true, something beautiful and good. Courage and strength in the face of adversity. Virtue without flaw.

MAUDE But this one had a flaw.

LIONEL It wasn't that it had a flaw.

MAUDE It was that it was a forgery.

LIONEL We all have flaws.

MAUDE A fake.

LIONEL	That statue was a major discovery.
MAUDE	Or a very expensive mistake.
LIONEL	It's easier to say something is fake than to prove something is real.
MAUDE	There you go.
LIONEL	But I knew! I knew! "Marble analysis". "Isotopic signature readings". Proved nothing. And that statue is still there. On public display at that Museum! To this day!
MAUDE	But you're not.
LIONEL	I was made an example of!
MAUDE	You were fired.
LIONEL	But I was not wrong! (*Beat.*) I was betrayed.
MAUDE	By the statue?
LIONEL	Art is silent and true. It's people who . . .
MAUDE	Yeah.
LIONEL	I was eviscerated in the *New York Times*. "The 'Archbishop of Art' has been Defrocked". Crucified for the sins of my brothers: do you have any idea how many fakes are on display around the world, being touted as real? Don't believe what you see. There's bogus paper on every major work of art. Nobody's hands are clean.
MAUDE	Then why didn't you fight back?

LIONEL   I did. I sent a letter of outrage to *ArtForum* magazine.

MAUDE   Oh, give me a fucking break.

LIONEL   Don't you dare criticize. What do you know about it?

MAUDE   I know there comes a time when you gotta stand up for yourself. Take control. Life is like sex. You can either lay back and get screwed or you can get on top and ride the hell out of it.

(*He stares at her.*)

LIONEL   I have no idea how that analogy pertains to what I'm –

MAUDE   Don't let assholes push you around. When you know you're right, never quit!

LIONEL   Enough! My wife tore into me, thank you very much. Ripped me apart. Day in and day out. I didn't have "the stuff." I was "weak," "afraid," "self-destructing."

MAUDE   She sounds like a keeper.

LIONEL   She . . .

(*Stops himself. Slugs down his drink. Silence.*)

MAUDE   We think someone is one thing . . . turns out they're not.

(*The moment hangs in the air.*)

LIONEL	Years before all this happened, after we first married – one morning – my wife brought home this ancient Chinese urn she acquired from a dealer. She loved ancient pottery.
MAUDE	My idea of ancient pottery is the tupperware I still have from 1981.
LIONEL	This urn was 960 BC. Unglazed. Stanniferous enamel. I knew it was fake. The moment I saw it. The shape. The typography. It was all wrong. I have a sixth sense about these things. I told my wife to remove it. She said no. She didn't care. It made no difference to her if it was real or not. No one would know. She displayed it anyway. Against my order. In the living room of our apartment. The very center of our home. This thing. This object. On a white alabaster pedestal. It was a lie. I couldn't go into the living room. I had to find alternate routes to get over to the kitchen because walking into that living room was like picking up a dagger and jabbing it into my . . . (*Breathes.*)
MAUDE	You and your wife? You still . . . ?
	(*He shakes his head.*)
LIONEL	She was revealed to be less than what I appraised her to be. Too often what seems to be superior turns out to be bogus. (*A cloud passes over his face. Pours himself another drink.*) A real work of art lives. An imitation is dead. It fools you temporarily. But living with it day in and day out? The deadness soon becomes hateful.
MAUDE	And the real thing?

LIONEL   One is filled and uplifted by the life that created it. In my years at the Met I must have examined fifty thousand works. In all fields. Forty percent were fake. Forgery is as old as art itself. The world wants to be fooled.

MAUDE   Except you.

LIONEL   I was fooled once. Never again.

            (MAUDE *eyes* LIONEL.)

MAUDE   That painting is real.

LIONEL   No. It's not.

MAUDE   So you're gonna check "no" on your form?

LIONEL   Absolutely.

            (*Beat. Then* MAUDE *moves in close to him. A sly little wink.*)

MAUDE   (*suggestive*) Are you sure . . . there isn't anything I can do . . . to change your mind?

            (LIONEL *stares at her. Aghast.*)

LIONEL   I beg your pardon?

            (*She grins at him.*)

MAUDE   Why don't you tell your driver outside to get lost? Circle the block a few times?

            (*He is horrified.*)

LIONEL   (*afraid to ask*) What are you suggesting?

MAUDE   I'm suggesting . . . (*Easing closer to him.*) Maybe all you need . . . is a little convincing.

           (*She winks at him. He stares at her. Appalled.*)

LIONEL   Are you out of your mind?

MAUDE   What's the matter?

LIONEL   You're drunk.

MAUDE   I better be. You think I'd smoke your pole sober?

LIONEL   You are the most crude, vulgar woman I have ever –

MAUDE   I need you to say that the painting is real.

LIONEL   Never.

MAUDE   Say it.

LIONEL   I'd be lying.

MAUDE   So lie.

LIONEL   Well, I'm sorry but I have a higher moral standard than you.

MAUDE   Oh, bite me.

LIONEL   Bite you?

MAUDE   That painting is a major find.

LIONEL   It is empty and worthless!

MAUDE	Says the ex-Museum Director.
LIONEL	I have expert intuition.
MAUDE	Your intuition is no better than mine.
LIONEL	What educated intuitions could you possibly have?
MAUDE	I get sudden flare-ups.
LIONEL	I'm not talking hot flashes.
MAUDE	I get hunches and gut feelings too, asshole.
LIONEL	Lovely.
MAUDE	I can sense things. Same as you. Common sense.
LIONEL	Common being the operative word.
MAUDE	I'm smarter than you think.
LIONEL	(*savage*) So am I. How much higher education have you had?
MAUDE	None of your fucking business.
LIONEL	You are uneducated and uninformed.
MAUDE	I know what I know!
LIONEL	(*brutal, ripping into her*) That painting will never be real just because you want it to be! Do you understand? You are ignorant! And a fool!
MAUDE	I am NOT STUPID!

LIONEL   (*savage*) You ARE! For BELIEVING in something that's BEYOND YOUR UNDERSTANDING!

(*Silence.* LIONEL *sets down his drink.*)

LIONEL   I've had enough.

(*He grabs his briefcase.*)

MAUDE   I was sitting in here watching *Law and Order* with my old friend Howard about a year ago.

LIONEL   This consultation is over.

MAUDE   Howard is retired. Used to be a detective. In San Bernadino.

LIONEL   I am leaving.

MAUDE   I had already mailed off my application to your Foundation. Waiting to hear back.

LIONEL   My office will contact you with my findings.

MAUDE   I've known Howard a long time. Ever since his wife died and he moved out this way. Howard's a gentleman. Never comes on to me. Never lays a hand on me.

LIONEL   Imagine the self-restraint.

MAUDE   We watch *Law and Order*. And I swear to God: Howard can always figure out who did it by the second commercial. And he's always right. Every time. He's a genius.

LIONEL   Mrs Gutman.

MAUDE   So one night – about a year ago – we're watching *Law and Order*. And I say to him, "Howard, I got to figure out a way to prove that fucking painting is a Pollock." So he says to me, "Treat the painting like a homicide."

(*She grabs a bizarre-looking magnifying glass.*)

So Howard grabs this magnifying glass. He walks over to the painting. I say, "What the fuck are you doing?" He says, "Rule one in homicide. Examine the body." He goes like this . . .

(*She holds the magnifying glass up to one eye and sticks her face up to the painting, inches away, and slowly examines it in long, slow lines – up and down.*)

LIONEL   Mrs Gutman.

MAUDE   Up and down . . .

LIONEL   Mrs Gutman.

MAUDE   Up . . .

LIONEL   Mrs Gutman.

MAUDE   and down . . . Felt like hours.

LIONEL   You're telling me.

MAUDE   Know what he found?

LIONEL   I can't imagine.

MAUDE   Nothing. Not a fucking thing.

LIONEL   Mrs Gutman. I am done playing charades
            with you.

MAUDE   Then. Howard turns the painting over . . . (*She
            turns the painting around, the canvas back
            now showing.*) That's when he finds . . . (*She
            points to a tiny paint smudge on the back of
            the canvas.*) That.

LIONEL   And what is that supposed to be?

MAUDE   That is a fingerprint. (*Silence.*) A
            fingerprint of Jackson Pollock.

            (MAUDE *grins. Pours herself a drink.* LIONEL
            *puts down his briefcase. Moves close to
            the canvas. Puts his face up to the smudge.
            Stares closely at it.*)

LIONEL   It is not.

MAUDE   Yes, it is.

LIONEL   How do you know?

MAUDE   Howard is a connoisseur.

            (LIONEL *glares at her.*)

LIONEL   An elderly beer-swilling widower from San
            Bernadino is not a fingerprint expert.

            (*She goes to a shelf. Pulls out a cardboard
            file box.*)

MAUDE   So Howard runs home. Comes back. Brings
            all these weird-looking tools with him.
            Scientific stuff. A microscope. Scalpel to
            take paint samples. Tweezers. This is his
            report.

(She hands it to him. He reads.)

LIONEL
"The painting is executed in high level gloss emulsion enamel and an acrylic resin paint –"

MAUDE
– the kind Pollock used.

LIONEL
"On stretched white cotton canvas, also called cotton duck –"

MAUDE
– the kind Pollock used.

LIONEL
(to MAUDE*)* Will you stop that? *(Continues reading.)* "I collected four scrapings of paint from the folded-over edge of the canvas with a surgical probe for later analyses. I collected six samples of hair and fibre embedded in the paint layer. The hair samples appear to be human, dark brown in color. The fingerprint was discovered on the verso".

MAUDE
That means the back.

LIONEL
"It was deposited with a fingertip that was coated with paint of various colors."

MAUDE
He also brought a fancy camera.

LIONEL
(reads) "The print was photographed by a high-powered digital camera with a macro lens at 1:1 reproduction ratio with a medical ring flash unit".

(MAUDE pulls a sheet of paper from the folder.)

MAUDE
This is Howard's photo of the fingerprint.

(He looks at it. Unimpressed.)

LIONEL	It could be anybody's.
MAUDE	But it's not.
LIONEL	There is no official record of Pollock's print.
MAUDE	I know that.
LIONEL	No fingerprint. Never arrested. Although, in a few cases, he should have been.
MAUDE	Me and Howard drove out to my brother's house. He showed me the website of the Museum of Modern Art. (*Shoots him a look.*) That's in New York City. On their website. Click on "archives". They got fancy hi-res digital photos of famous paintings. So art students can study them. You can zoom in real close. Real fucking close. It's amazing. See each tiny brush stroke. Each micro-dot of paint. (*Pulling out a sheet of paper.*) From the website.

(*He glances at it. Knows it immediately.*)

LIONEL	It's "Lavender Mist".
MAUDE	Pollock's painting. Famous. He got down on his hands and knees when he painted it. Actually stuck his fucking hands on it. His fingers in the paint. On the Museum website, when you zoom in super-duper close, right there – you can see . . .

(*She displays another photo.*)

MAUDE	Pollock's fingerprint. In blue paint.

(MAUDE *takes the two sheets of photo paper over to a lamp on a table.*)

MAUDE	Follow me. You'll learn something.
	(LIONEL *follows. She switches on the lamp. Holds one of the photos up to the lamp.*)
MAUDE	Pollock's fingerprint on "Lavender Mist". (*Holds up the other photo next to it.*) The fingerprint from my painting.
	(*Now overlapping one behind the other.*)
	Wait for it . . .
	(*Holds them up to the light.* MAUDE *and* LIONEL *stare at it.* LIONEL *doesn't move. Frozen. She nods to Howard's report, still in* LIONEL'S *hand. He reads from the report.*)
LIONEL	"Twelve characteristics of the two fingerprints appear identical: seven bifurcations, three small islands, and two ridge endings. The correspondence of twelve characteristics is confirmation that Pollock's fingerprint on "Lavender Mist" was left by the same finger as the fingerprint on the back of the painting. They are one and the same."
	(*She grins. He doesn't move.* LIONEL *peers at the photo of the "fingerprint". A long silence.*)
LIONEL	Well, I don't believe that at all.
MAUDE	What do you mean?
LIONEL	I don't believe it.
MAUDE	How can you not believe it?

LIONEL	I choose not to believe it.
MAUDE	You have to believe it.
LIONEL	What is that fingerprint supposed to mean?
MAUDE	What do you mean, what's it mean? It means.
LIONEL	I don't understand fingerprints.
MAUDE	What's to understand? Don't you watch *Law and Order*?
LIONEL	A fingerprint proves nothing.
MAUDE	It's is the fingerprint of Jackson Pollack!
LIONEL	You assume. You don't know!
MAUDE	It's the same fingerprint as the one in the famous painting!
LIONEL	You don't know who's print that is.
MAUDE	He painted it. Who's fingerprint would it be? The Dali Lama?
LIONEL	Pollock was never fingerprinted. Therefore, any fingerprint can not be verified as his beyond a reasonable doubt.
MAUDE	Now you sound like all the other . . .
LIONEL	What are you trying to do with this fingerprint business? Set me up? Trap me?
MAUDE	Of course not.
LIONEL	Why didn't you tell me about this before?

MAUDE	I want you to say the thing is real on your own. Not influence you.
LIONEL	Not influence me? You were offering me sex. What do you call that?
MAUDE	Encouragement.
LIONEL	This fingerprint – whomever it belongs to – is worthless.
MAUDE	It is proof!
LIONEL	Of what? That Howard likes *Law and Order*? His scientific opinion is meaningless to me. You want to submit fingerprint evidence? Hire an objective, professional, fully certified specialist who's opinion is recognized and respected by the international art community.
MAUDE	An expert.
LIONEL	That's right.
MAUDE	I don't have the money to hire a fancy guy like that.
LIONEL	Then – as you and Howard might say – you are "shit out of luck".
MAUDE	Not if you do it.
LIONEL	Do what?
MAUDE	Get the fingerprint expert.
LIONEL	Are you serious?
MAUDE	You must know a shitload.

LIONEL   I can't do that.

MAUDE   Make the phone call. Right now.

LIONEL   Mrs Gutman.

(She holds up a colorful, bizarre-looking telephone.)

MAUDE   Here. Use my phone.

LIONEL   I'll do no such thing.

MAUDE   (*the phone*) It works. Don't be scared. You just gotta jiggle the –

LIONEL   I have a phone, Mrs Gutman.

MAUDE   Well get on that sucker, pal. Start dialing the Foundation.

LIONEL   And tell them what?

MAUDE   To hire a fingerprint specialist. One certified and approved. Get his ass over here.

LIONEL   I am not going to do that.

MAUDE   Why not?

LIONEL   I can not become personally involved. As I said at the start, I have no personal interest in this painting.

MAUDE   We both know that's bullshit. Make the call.

LIONEL   It's simply not done.

MAUDE	Lots of things aren't done until someobdy does it.
LIONEL	That's not how it works, Mrs Gutman. The onus is on you. It's not the Foundation's responsibility to pay for proper testing on every case that comes along.
MAUDE	My painting is not every case.
LIONEL	To you. The Foundation sees your painting otherwise. Or, to be more accurate, will never see it at all.
MAUDE	Then fuck the Foundation.
LIONEL	Excuse me?
MAUDE	Don't you want to know the truth?
LIONEL	I already know.
MAUDE	Prove it. Make the call. Order the expert. Do it. If it's a fake? Case closed.
LIONEL	I will not further involve the Foundation.
MAUDE	What are you afraid of?
LIONEL	I will not lower my standing with the Foundation by indulging your pathetic masquerade of make-believe.
MAUDE	You're scared.
LIONEL	I am not.
MAUDE	Terrified.
LIONEL	Of what?

MAUDE	That your own fingerprint guy will prove you wrong. You care more about your reputation than the truth.
LIONEL	That is professionally insulting and absurd.
MAUDE	Am I being impolite? How's this. You fucking art assholes are all alike. Every goddamn one-of-ya!
LIONEL	All alike?

(*She mimes an imaginary "telephone".*)

MAUDE	"Hello? Elliot Knightsbridge Art Gallery? I have a masterpiece by Jackson Pollack I bought at a thrift store for three bucks and I" – *Click!* "Hello, Pressman-Weiss Fine Art Boutique? I know it may sound crazy, but guess what? I found a long-lost Jackson Pollack worth millions I found in a junk shop and I" – *Click!* Even the asshole from Arabella Art Gallery. He came over. Saw the painting, I showed him the fingerprint. He stood right there, where you're standing now.
LIONEL	And what did he say?
MAUDE	That I was out of my fucking mind.
LIONEL	Case closed.
MAUDE	But he's wrong.
LIONEL	You've had other experts over here? And say exactly the same thing that I'm telling you now?
MAUDE	I've had it up to here with "experts".

LIONEL	Then what am I doing here?
MAUDE	You're my last fucking chance. My only hope.
LIONEL	You are looking for hope where there is none.
MAUDE	Don't you believe in anything?
LIONEL	I believe in my scholarship. I believe in my learning. My esthetic eye and expertise. I believe in that deep inner voice that tells me when something is true and when it is false.
MAUDE	Well, I hear voices, too, you know.
LIONEL	No doubt.
MAUDE	It's still just your opinion.
LIONEL	Yes! But my opinion means something! Yours does not!
	(MAUDE *stands there. Dazed. Unable to move. Like a prizefighter who's taken a blow to the head.*)
MAUDE	Fine.
	(*She goes to the kitchen counter. Grabs a large knife.*)
LIONEL	What are you doing?
MAUDE	Does it matter?
LIONEL	Be careful with that.
MAUDE	Why?

LIONEL	Put that down.
MAUDE	I'm unimportant. Right? Amount to nothin'?
LIONEL	Now, wait a minute.

(*She holds the knife, gazing at it.*)

MAUDE	My husband used to say, "Maude, you're just a fucking waste of skin."
LIONEL	Put down the knife, Mrs Gutman.
MAUDE	"You ain't done nothin' worth doin' in this world."
LIONEL	Mrs Gutman . . .
MAUDE	"Ain't nobody gonna miss you when you're gone."
LIONEL	Put it down.
MAUDE	He was right. You said it yourself. Me and this painting – both of us – are worthless. Right?
LIONEL	I didn't say that.
MAUDE	Worthless junk. Without value. No reason to exist. So? Who gives a shit? Might as well . . . (*She raises the big knife above her head.*) – SLASH THE PAINTING UP! (*And – lunges at the painting!*)
MAUDE	(*screaming*) Aaaaaaaaaaaaaahhhhhhhhhhh!

(LIONEL *leaps forward – hurling himself at her!*)

LIONEL	*NO! DON'T!*
	(*He grabs the knife.*)
MAUDE	*I CAN'T TAKE IT ANY MORE!*
LIONEL	*GIVE ME THAT KNIFE!*
MAUDE	*GET YOUR FUCKING HANDS OFF ME!*
LIONEL	*DON'T DO IT!*
	(*They tussle back-and-forth.*)
MAUDE	(*shrieking*) *I'LL SLASH THE FUCKER UP!*
LIONEL	*JESUS CHRIST, WOMAN!*
MAUDE	*THROW THE SHREDS OUT THE WINDOW!*
LIONEL	*ARE YOU OUT OF YOUR MIND?*
	(*They struggle, they wrestle! Wild! Frantic! Knock over furniture! Her bizarre household objects flying everywhere!*)
MAUDE	Ow!
LIONEL	Ouch!
	(*They tumble together to the floor. Finally – he yanks the knife from her. They both remain on the floor. Collapsed. Exhausted. Panting. Out of breath. Silence.* MAUDE *grins.*)
MAUDE	So you do think its real.

(Silence. He peers at her. They remain on the floor. Panting heavily. Out of breath. Sweating.)

LIONEL: I think . . . I'm having . . . a heart attack. *(Gasping for breath.)* I am too old for this. I have a bad back. If you see . . . any small round objects on the floor . . . they may be my vertebra. *(Glares at her.)* You are insane. An insane person. You know that?

MAUDE: Pollock was put in the crazy asylum. Why not me?

(The room is in shambles. Furniture knocked over, broken stuff everywhere, littering the floor.)

LIONEL: We've made a mess of your place. Your things.

MAUDE: It's only junk.

(Something on the floor catches her eye.)

MAUDE: Oh, no . . .

(She crawls on her hands and knees across the floor. Picks up a broken picture frame. A photo inside. Glass shattered.)

LIONEL: What is it?

MAUDE: My boy. My Eddie.

(She tenderly picks the bits of broken glass from the frame.)

LIONEL: Can it be repaired?

MAUDE	No. Gone.
LIONEL	I saw the picture earlier.
MAUDE	Isn't he handsome?
LIONEL	Yes.
MAUDE	Mothers always think their sons are handsome.
LIONEL	How old is he there?
MAUDE	Nineteen.
LIONEL	How old is he now?
MAUDE	You have any?
LIONEL	No. My wife and I opted against having children. She wanted them. I was resistant.
MAUDE	Why?
LIONEL	For me, having children would require . . .
MAUDE	Having sex with your wife?
LIONEL	There was that. (*Then.*) My parents divorced when I was six. (*Then.*) Parents . . . the wrong parent . . . can destroy a boy's belief in himself.
MAUDE	I know.
	(*Silence*).
MAUDE	(*gazing at the photograph*) Everything was hard for my Eddie. Ever since he was a little boy. Reading. Writing. Everyday life was a

	struggle. My Eddie was born with too big an engine inside him. Too big a heart for this world. A very sensitive boy. Whenever I went to the market – or was gone for something – he would run up to me. "Did you miss me, Mom?" Always look to me. Want my approval. We had this thing, you know? When he was a boy? Me and my Eddie. Your boy . . . it's like your heart is outside your body, walking around.
LIONEL	His father?
MAUDE	Was a mean son of a bitch. When he was drinking. Which was always. He'd get wild drunk. Pick on Eddie. Call him all kinds of shit. Say he was dumb. He wasn't dumb. He was different. But when the man you look up to tells you you're nothin' every day of your life you can't help but grow up believin' it.
LIONEL	The image I am forming of your husband is not an altogether . . .
MAUDE	He was somethin' when I married him. Good lookin'. Talked a good game. Knew better than everyone. Smarter. Superior. You knew he was goin' places. Turns out the only place he went was the corner bar and that couch. Sat there all day. Getting drunk. Watch the Hunting Channel. Marryin' me, having Eddie, ruined his life.
LIONEL	Now he's gone.
MAUDE	One day he just grabbed his shit and left. Happiest day of my life. Standing outside this trailer with my Eddie. Watching the dust behind that man's pickup get smaller and smaller as it disappeared down Highway 12. But the damage had been done. Eddie

BAKERSFIELD MIST 63

was twenty-two. Angry. Hurting. Drunk most of the time. Beer in the morning. Bourbon at night. A wild one. Wrestling with himself. A dark scowl on his face. Like he was always looking into a hard-driven rain. Didn't talk to nobody. Not even me. He'd sit in here for hours. Not saying nothing. There was this storm inside my boy. (*Peers at the painting. The violent tornado of color.*) Just like that painting. Like that. (*She fires up a Camel.*) One hot afternoon. August. He drinks a six pack of Coors. Stumbles out the front door. Gets in his black Mustang. Revs it up. Off he went. Gone. (*Agonizes. Silence.*) They found his body twisted up in the car. Neck broken. His car crumpled up on the side of the highway like an empty pack of cigarettes. (*Stubs out her Camel.*)

(MAUDE *opens a drawer. Reaches in. Pulls out her .45. Sets it on the table in front of her. She stares at the gun.* LIONEL *eyes her. Terrified. Not moving.*)

MAUDE   Everything just goes black. You can't see anything. Like falling into a black hole. Down, down, down. Gone. Can't get out. I read in an art book that white is the absence of color. You probably know that. White is the absence of color. But black . . . black is all the colors. Mixed together. All at once. Everything. Becoming nothing.

(*She raises the gun to her head.*)

MAUDE   The last year he was alive Pollock painted only in black. His only color: black. All that color – gone. (*The gun now at her temple. She pulls back the hammer.*) Then Pollock got in his Oldsmobile. And stepped on the gas . . .

(*She pulls the trigger.* LIONEL *jumps! Click. Nothing happens.* LIONEL *exhales.*)

LIONEL (*relieved*) Oh . . . my . . . God . . .

(*He collapses into a chair, shaken.* MAUDE *sighs. She examines the gun. Looks at it. Long silence.*)

MAUDE Me and Roberta never did find the bullets to this thing.

(LIONEL *stares at her.*)

LIONEL You knew there were no bullets in that gun.

MAUDE There will be. One day.

LIONEL You did that on purpose.

MAUDE Scared ya, didn't I?

(LIONEL *eyes her.*)

LIONEL I underestimated you. My first impression of you was completely inaccurate.

MAUDE See? You "blink", you miss me. (*Then.*) Tell me now what my painting is worth.

LIONEL I told you. I can't offer an appraisal.

(MAUDE *rises. Starts picking up the pieces of her broken home.*)

MAUDE Don't matter. I already got one.

LIONEL	An appraisal?
MAUDE	An offer.
LIONEL	What?
MAUDE	For the painting. Somebody wants to buy it.
LIONEL	Who?
MAUDE	Some businessman. In India.
LIONEL	How'd he hear about it?
MAUDE	My brother. On line. Behind my back.
LIONEL	You have an offer? A serious offer?
MAUDE	I'd say it's serious. I got the letter. Over there. In that can.

(*As* MAUDE *continues to pick up –* LIONEL *goes to the tin canister. Opens it. Pulls out the letter. Starts to reads it. His jaw drops.*)

LIONEL	Two million dollars?
MAUDE	No questions asked.

(*He skims through the letter.*)

LIONEL	He's not requiring any paperwork.
MAUDE	Nope.
LIONEL	No certificate. Nothing.
MAUDE	He'll just buy it. Cash. Done. Boom. That's the offer.

LIONEL   This is unbelievable.

MAUDE   That's the offer.

LIONEL   And you said?

MAUDE   I haven't.

LIONEL   Why not?

(*She looks away.*)

LIONEL   Are you out of your mind? Take the money.

MAUDE   No.

LIONEL   For God's sake, why not?

MAUDE   It's worth so much more.

LIONEL   Two million dollars.

MAUDE   Pollock never settled. No matter what. Even when he was broke. Neither will I.

(LIONEL *doesn't move. A long pause. Then he sits opposite her. Peers into her eyes. Very gentle. Earnest.*)

LIONEL   Maude . . . Maude . . . Listen to me . . . (*Sincere. Very serious.*) Maude . . . please . . . take the money.

(*Silence.*)

MAUDE   (*almost a whisper*) I can't.

LIONEL   Take the money. You could move somewhere nice, buy a new house.

MAUDE   This is not about money.

LIONEL   Why put yourself through all this?

MAUDE   I have no choice. Never did. One day my boy is gone. And then, one afternoon, this thing arrives. Out of nowhere. I didn't find this painting. This painting found me. The world needs to know its true worth. Its true value. I'm seeing this through to the end. I can't explain. Some things you can't say in words. I'm not the expert. But isn't that what art is supposed to do?

(*He gazes at her.*)

LIONEL   (*the simple truth*) Yes. Yes it is. (*Then.*) You can't fight this forever. One day your window of opportunity will close.

(*She looks to him.*)

MAUDE   (*quietly*) That's why I need you. (*A breath.*) Please. (*She clasps his hand.*) I am begging you. (*Quiet.*) I need your blessing. A blessing from the Pope. Please. Give the painting your blessing. Say that it's real.

(*He stares at her. At the painting. Silence.*)

LIONEL   The Rand Corporation did an experiment. They took a world-class violinist, Joshua Bell, and dressed him up in homeless clothes. They placed him and his 3.5 million dollar Stradivarius down in the subway. A tin cup at his feet. He played Bach. Magnificently. The most intricate pieces ever written. All day. You know what people did? Brushed right by. Didn't notice. Never stopped. Never knowing they were ignoring the most glorious music ever written played by one of the greatest violinists in the entire world. (*A pause.*) Nobody knows anything.

(*Beat. She looks to him.*)

MAUDE   Not even you?

(*He peers at her.*)

LIONEL   Take the two million.

(*Silence. He opens his folder. Takes out his form.* MAUDE *halts. Doesn't move.*)

MAUDE   You're marking your form now.

(*He looks to her.*)

LIONEL   (*quietly*) Yes, I am.

(*He marks a check on the form. Stands before her. Neither of them move.*)

MAUDE   Which is it? "Yes" or "No"?

(*He hands her the form. She takes it. Reads it. Looks at the box he marked on the form. Her face drops. She sits. Motionless.* LIONEL *takes the form from her hand. Puts the form in his folder. The folder in his briefcase. Snaps it shut. Click. He heads for the door. Stops. Turns.*)

LIONEL   The painting is not authentic. (*A gentle look to her.*) But you . . . (*Silence. A long pause. Then . . . trying to give her something.*) Arete. (*Gazes at her.*) But you don't need an expert to tell you that.

	(*A moment.*)
MAUDE	(*not looking at him*) Get out.
	(*He doesn't move.*)
	Get the fuck out. Now.
	(LIONEL *exits. Out the door. Gone.* MAUDE *sits. Alone. Outside, the sound of the limousine door opening. Slamming shut. The limousine starting up.* MAUDE *bolts to the door, flings it open.*)
MAUDE	(*calling outside to him*) Go on! Get out of here! Get the fuck outta here! (*As she screams.*) I AM NOT GIVING UP! YOU HEAR ME? THIS THING IS *REAL* AND I AM NOT GIVING UP!
	(*Sound of the limousine pulling away. Silence.* MAUDE *slowly closes the door. She is alone. With the painting. She sits. Pours herself a drink. Fires up another Camel. Suddenly – The wind picks up outside. The beer bottle wind chimes suddenly move, come to life and rattle. Outside the sun ducks behind a cloud. In the room, the light changes, moves . . . The sunlight lands on the painting a certain way – The painting glows. Alive.* MAUDE *grins. Raises her glass to the painting and "toasts" it as the lights fade to black. The End.*)